FRANCIS FRITH'S

KENT REVISITED

PHOTOGRAPHIC MEMORIES

MELODY RYALL is an award-winning journalist and writer with experience in newspapers, magazines and broadcasting. She has edited newspapers in east Kent, north Kent and south-east London, and is a graduate of the University of Kent. She is currently Group Editor of Kentish Times Newspapers (Archant London) She lives in a village near Canterbury with her two cats.

FRANCIS FRITH'S
PHOTOGRAPHIC MEMORIES

KENT REVISITED

PHOTOGRAPHIC MEMORIES

MELODY RYALL

First published in the United Kingdom in 2006 by
The Francis Frith Collection

Hardback Edition 2006
ISBN 1-85937-450-6

British Library Cataloguing in Publication Data

Kent Revisited - Photographic Memories
Melody Ryall
ISBN 1-85937-450-6

The Francis Frith Collection
Frith's Barn, Teffont,
Salisbury, Wiltshire SP3 5QP
Tel: +44 (0) 1722 716 376
Email: info@francisfrith.co.uk
www.francisfrith.com

Printed and bound in Great Britain

Front Cover: **CRANBROOK**, *Stone Street 1906* 56971t
Frontispiece: **DOVER**, *Marine Parade 1892* 31418

*The colour-tinting is for illustrative purposes only, and is not intended to be
historically accurate*

Aerial photographs reproduced under licence from
Simmons Aerofilms Limited.
Historical Ordnance Survey maps reproduced under licence from Homecheck.co.uk
Every attempt has been made to contact copyright holders of illustrative material. We will
be happy to give full acknowledgement in future editions for any items not credited. Any
information should be directed to The Francis Frith Collection.

AS WITH ANY HISTORICAL DATABASE THE FRITH ARCHIVE IS CONSTANTLY BEING
CORRECTED AND IMPROVED AND THE PUBLISHERS WOULD WELCOME INFORMATION ON
OMISSIONS OR INACCURACIES

CONTENTS

FRANCIS FRITH
VICTORIAN PIONEER

FRANCIS FRITH, founder of the world-famous photographic archive, was a complex and multi-talented man. A devout Quaker and a highly successful Victorian businessman, he was philosophical by nature and pioneering in outlook.

By 1855 he had already established a wholesale grocery business in Liverpool, and sold it for the astonishing sum of £200,000, which is the equivalent today of over £15,000,000. Now a very rich man, he was able to indulge his passion for travel. As a child he had pored over travel books written by early explorers, and his fancy and imagination had been stirred by family holidays to the sublime mountain regions of Wales and Scotland. 'What lands of spirit-stirring and enriching scenes and places!' he had written. He was to return to these scenes of grandeur in later years to 'recapture the thousands of vivid and tender memories', but with a different purpose. Now in his thirties, and captivated by the new science of photography, Frith set out on a series of

pioneering journeys up the Nile and to the Near East that occupied him from 1856 until 1860.

INTRIGUE AND EXPLORATION

These far-flung journeys were packed with intrigue and adventure. In his life story, written when he was sixty-three, Frith tells of being held captive by bandits, and of fighting 'an awful midnight battle to the very point of surrender with a deadly pack of hungry, wild dogs'. Wearing flowing Arab costume, Frith arrived at Akaba by camel sixty years before Lawrence of Arabia, where he encountered 'desert princes and rival sheikhs, blazing with jewel-hilted swords'.

He was the first photographer to venture beyond the sixth cataract of the Nile. Africa was still the mysterious 'Dark Continent', and Stanley and Livingstone's historic meeting was a decade into the future. The conditions for picture taking confound belief. He laboured for hours in his wicker dark-room in the sweltering heat of the desert, while the volatile chemicals fizzed dangerously in their trays. Back in London he exhibited his photographs and was 'rapturously cheered' by members of the Royal Society. His reputation as a photographer was made overnight.

VENTURE OF A LIFE-TIME

Characteristically, Frith quickly spotted the opportunity to create a new business as a specialist publisher of photographs. He lived in an era of immense and sometimes violent change.

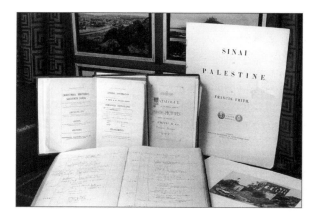

For the poor in the early part of Victoria's reign work was exhausting and the hours long, and people had precious little free time to enjoy themselves. Most had no transport other than a cart or gig at their disposal, and rarely travelled far beyond the boundaries of their own town or village. However, by the 1870s the railways had threaded their way across the country, and Bank Holidays and half-day Saturdays had been made obligatory by Act of Parliament. All of a sudden the working man and his family were able to enjoy days out and see a little more of the world.

With typical business acumen, Francis Frith foresaw that these new tourists would enjoy having souvenirs to commemorate their days out. In 1860 he married Mary Ann Rosling and set out on a new career: his aim was to photograph every city, town and village in Britain. For the next thirty years he travelled the country by train and by pony and trap, producing fine photographs of seaside resorts and beauty spots that were keenly bought by millions of Victorians. These prints were painstakingly pasted into family albums and pored over during the dark nights of winter, rekindling precious memories of summer excursions.

THE RISE OF FRITH & CO

Frith's studio was soon supplying retail shops all over the country. To meet the demand he gathered about him a small team of photographers, and published the work of independent artist-photographers of the calibre of Roger Fenton and Francis Bedford. In order to gain some understanding of the scale of Frith's business one only has to look at the catalogue issued by Frith & Co in 1886: it runs to some 670 pages, listing not only many thousands of views of the British Isles but also many photographs of most European countries, and China, Japan, the USA and Canada - note the sample page shown on page 9 from the hand-written Frith & Co ledgers recording the pictures. By 1890 Frith had created the greatest specialist photographic publishing company in the world, with over 2,000 sales outlets - more than the combined number that Boots and WH Smith have today! The picture on the next page shows the Frith & Co display board at Ingleton in the Yorkshire Dales (left of window). Beautifully constructed with a mahogany frame and gilt inserts, it could display up to a dozen local scenes.

POSTCARD BONANZA

The ever-popular holiday postcard we know today took many years to develop. In 1870 the Post Office issued the first plain cards, with a pre-printed stamp on one face. In 1894 they allowed other publishers' cards to be sent through the mail with an attached adhesive halfpenny stamp. Demand grew rapidly, and in 1895 a new size of postcard was permitted called the court card, but there was little room for illustration. In 1899, a year after Frith's death, a new card measuring 5.5 x 3.5 inches became the standard format, but it was not until 1902 that the divided back came into being, so that the address and message could be on one face and a full-size illustration on the other. Frith & Co were in the vanguard of postcard development: Frith's sons Eustace and Cyril continued their father's monumental task, expanding the number of views offered to the public and recording more and more places in Britain, as the coasts and countryside were opened up to mass travel.

Francis Frith had died in 1898 at his villa in Cannes, his great project still growing. The archive he created continued in business for another seventy years. By 1970 it contained over a third of a million pictures showing 7,000 British towns and villages.

FRANCIS FRITH'S LEGACY

Frith's legacy to us today is of immense significance and value, for the magnificent archive of evocative photographs he created provides a unique record of change in the cities, towns and villages throughout Britain over a century and more. Frith and his fellow studio photographers revisited locations many times down the years to update their views, compiling for us an enthralling and colourful pageant of British life and character.

We are fortunate that Frith was dedicated to recording the minutiae of everyday life, for it is this sheer wealth of visual data, the painstaking chronicle of changes in dress, transport, street layouts, buildings, housing, engineering and landscape that captivates us so much today. His remarkable images offer us a powerful link with the past and with the lives of our ancestors.

THE VALUE OF THE ARCHIVE TODAY

Computers have now made it possible for Frith's many thousands of images to be accessed almost instantly. Frith's images are increasingly used as visual resources, by social historians, by researchers into genealogy and ancestry, by architects and town planners, and by teachers involved in local history projects.

In addition, the archive offers every one of us an opportunity to examine the places where we and our families have lived and worked down the years. Highly successful in Frith's own era, the archive is now, a century and more on, entering a new phase of popularity. Historians consider the Francis Frith Collection to be of prime national importance. It is the only archive of its kind remaining in private ownership. Francis Frith's archive is now housed in an historic timber barn in the beautiful village of Teffont in Wiltshire. Its founder would not recognize the archive office as it is today. In place of the many thousands of dusty boxes containing glass plate negatives and an all-pervading odour of photographic chemicals, there are now ranks of computer screens. He would be amazed to watch his images travelling round the world at unimaginable speeds through internet lines.

The archive's future is both bright and exciting. Francis Frith, with his unshakeable belief in making photographs available to the greatest number of people, would undoubtedly approve of what is being done today with his lifetime's work. His photographs depicting our shared past are now bringing pleasure and enlightenment to millions around the world a century and more after his death.

KENT
AN INTRODUCTION

AS one of the biggest and arguably the most diverse counties in England, Kent boasts a history as ripe as the apples that fall from its famous orchard trees. For a start there are the hop fields, vineyards, marshlands, ancient churches, two cathedrals, castles, stately homes, ports, agriculture and industries of merit, plus a host of famous sons and daughters.

So where did it all begin? A big question about a big county that stretches, twists and bends for miles and miles from the English Channel all the way to London and the Sussex borders. What a territorial challenge, then, for the two Saxon lords, Hengist and Horsa; early records reveal that they landed at Pegwell Bay in the fifth century. Evidence of their ambition to dominate Kent can be found, if legend is true, at Kit's Coty near Aylesford. It is here that ancient stones mark the burial site of a warrior who fought them and lost as they invaded his settlement. But as the county's white horse insignia, 'unconquered and untamed', goes back before their time here, so it

ROCHESTER, *The Castle and the Cathedral 1894* 34029

reveals that the locals were becoming used to the idea of yet another invasion, and adopted their own mantra for survival during the regular attacks from overseas visitors.

The Romans had marched in decades before the Saxons, and brought with them road building expertise and other areas of civilisation that left its mark on the county. Indeed, the remains of their hot baths can still be seen in Canterbury, along with evidence of a theatre built there in AD 290. The weed-covered remains of a castle at Richborough near Sandwich continues to arouse much archaeological interest today.

By the seventh century, though, the Saxons had made a significant impact on the landscape. One of the best places to see this today is in the village of Barfreston near Dover. The church here is reputed to be the most perfect example of Saxon architecture in England. This church, and other early evidence of Christian worship, must have been an encouragement of sorts to Augustine and his monks, who were sent from Italy to Canterbury in 597 by Pope Gregory to carry out the mammoth task of spreading the word of God to the English. This decision, supported by King Ethelbert and Queen Bertha, proved a world-shattering one, and over the years changed the lives of millions who had previously only paganism, warfare and folk ideologies upon which to depend for their spiritual well being. Queen Bertha, it is said, had begun worshipping at St Martin's Church in Canterbury years before Augustine arrived. This church, a sixth-century wonder, is believed to be England's oldest.

RAMSGATE, *The Parade and New Road 1901* 48028

During his stay in east Kent, Augustine, who became Canterbury Cathedral's first archbishop, lived with his fellow priests in Reculver, near Herne Bay.

Long after his death, in the Middle Ages the cathedral walls became witness to one of the world's most famous murders. In 1170 the archbishop, Thomas a Becket, was stabbed to death by four knights of Henry II. These men, fiercely loyal, had heard their king declare in frustration one day: 'Who will rid me of this turbulent priest?' and took it upon themselves to slay Thomas - a former friend and ally of Henry. They gathered at Saltwood Castle near Hythe hours before carrying out the deadly deed that still haunts Canterbury to this day.

Over the years, millions have flocked to the site of Becket's death in order to pay homage. Among the most famous to make the journey to Canterbury are of course the pilgrims. Their trek from Southwark to the cathedral city led them across the North Downs and parts of the Weald. Many of the routes they took are signposted across the county today as part of the Pilgrims' Way. The medieval writer Geoffrey Chaucer was so inspired by the idea that he wrote his famous 'Canterbury Tales' - a collection of poems about the everyday characters who took to the road and the hills to make for Canterbury. Parts of the cathedral we know today would have been there at the time of Chaucer, and in the village of Detling en route there is proof on ancient maps that the pilgrims stopped there for rest and refreshment before continuing towards the east.

On our own journey in this book through the Garden of England it is still possible to see almost 500 medieval buildings in the little town of Faversham. It was here

CANTERBURY, *West Gate 1890* 25695

12

that the brewer Shepherd Neame began life by maximising upon its prime position near to hop fields and clear spring water. The brewery remains today as Britain's oldest, and its regular tours attract hundreds of real ale fans throughout the year.

In the middle of the county we can still march through Union Street in Maidstone, where Wat Tyler and the peasants staged their revolt in 1381. The Civil War meant that the county was under siege yet again. Many towns offered Royalists safe houses. The last armed battle to take place on English soil is believed to have been the Courtenay Riots of 1838 at Dunkirk, near Faversham.

The beauty of Kent, with its rolling fields and spectacular houses, meant that there has always been a regular stream of royal visitors. Elizabeth I and Charles II enjoyed the east part of the county, and Henry VIII made regular visits to Hever Castle, the stunning childhood home of his second wife, Anne Boleyn. In the castle today visitors can see great paintings and other works of art, including a recently discovered portrait of Catherine Parr - the sixth wife of Henry, and a remarkable woman in her own right. Catherine is believed to be the first woman writer ever to be published, and a book of poetry she wrote became so popular that her success infuriated her royal husband, whose own book of hymns had not nearly as many fans!

Royal connections with Kent continued well into the 20th century. Queen Elizabeth II and

DYMCHURCH, *The Sands 1927* 80401

her husband Prince Philip have visited often, especially in Brabourne, near Ashford, home to the couple's dearest friends, Lord and Lady Brabourne. In Dartford towards the end of the last century the Queen cut the ribbon across an amazing new bridge across the River Thames, and in the 1960s her daughter Princess Anne enjoyed the education provided by the committed teachers at Benenden School. Prime ministers enjoy the county too, with one of Britain's most notable statesmen, Sir Winston Churchill, having a home at Chartwell near Westerham.

Meanwhile the sea and all its small relations that poured through Kent as rivers and estuaries played a huge part in the industrial welfare of the county. Chatham Dockyard was once home to Sir Francis Drake, and Admiral Nelson set off in the 'Victory' from here in 1865. (Fifty years later, in Crayford the Vickers aircraft factory was doing steady business during World War I supplying fighting machines to bring down the enemy in the air).

The marshlands of Old Romney and New Romney were home to smugglers of old. These bearded racketeers bringing rum and tobacco from Holland and France provided inspiration for Victorian novelists like Wilkie Collins and Russell Thorndike. Thorndike's Dr Syn stories, laced with Gothic overtones, offer the reader mystery and suspense set in the ancient stone homes and farms in and around the foggy marshland surrounding Dymchurch.

In this area generations of farmers have reared a hardy breed of sheep to weather the mercurial winds and rains that rampage across the marshes throughout the seasons. From there we can reach Folkestone, where fishing has remained a key industry, alongside the port of nearby Dover, where the ferry industry and Her Majesty's Customs and Excise have provided jobs for generations of local families.

In the 1950s, 60s, and 70s, many Londoners swarmed to Margate to enjoy its sandy charms, its bed and breakfast establishments, and the hurly burly of the big wheel and roller coaster rides at an entertainments park known as Dreamland. It was this seaside town which helped spark off a major new industry in Kent that is as important as the county's oast houses, orchards, castles, agriculture and cathedrals - tourism. With new and improving transport routes to the county like the Channel Tunnel, the new rail link, and the widening of the A2 in north Kent, the number of visitors arriving in the Garden of England increases every year. It is ironic to think, then, how long ago the people of Kent once fought off invaders. Today they reap the benefits of such high visitor numbers, and they have a reason to embrace their home county's popularity with pride. With so much to see, to enjoy and most importantly to learn here, Kent continues to flourish; it retains a unique identity of its own - an identity that plays a major part in the socio-economic and cultural welfare of England today.

A SECTION OF A COUNTY MAP OF KENT SHOWING CANTERBURY c1850

LOCKSBOTTOM, *The Village c1955* L328002

I wonder how long the two people on the left had been waiting for a bus to take them into Bromley? Although it looks as if this village had a grocer's shop, if residents wanted the big town experience it was necessary to travel a few miles. When this picture was taken, the local MP, Harold Macmillan, had just been appointed foreign secretary by Anthony Eden.

METROPOLITAN KENT

AT the top end of the very north west of the county sits a collection of towns and villages that in the latter half of the 20th century were embraced as London boroughs, even though their postal addresses retain 'Kent' in them. Although they have their own local councils, being so close to the capital means that the boroughs of Bromley and Bexley exude an atmosphere of urgency, influence and affluence. Towns like Bromley and Beckenham and large villages like Chislehurst boast large houses that belong to stockbrokers, celebrities, city whiz kids and lawyers. Metropolitan Kent is an area rich in history, and it has also been home to key businesses which enabled its communities to flourish and grow. In World War II the RAF base at Biggin Hill played a huge role in the Battle of Britain. It was in this area that aircraft manufacture, silk making, tannery, publishing, and fabric designing grew up in the 20th century, and helped to establish towns like Sidcup, Crayford, Erith, Bexleyheath, Welling, Orpington, Eltham and Beckenham. They are what locals call 'Kentish' towns - in other words, they are very much on the north side of the River Medway. Hence the old saying that people born here were Kentish Men, and those born south of the river were Men of Kent.

▲ **BROMLEY,** *The Broadway, High Street c1950* B226006

Around this time the former classics teacher of the town's high school, Miss Richmal Crompton, was famed for being the author of the Just William books. It is more than likely that as a Bromley town resident she bought her bread from the Hovis bakers, right, or visited Wymans shop nearby.

◄ **BROMLEY**
High Street 1948
B226009

A prosperous row of shops indicate the popularity of this desirable suburb so near to the capital. No doubt the watchmaker P H Ede, left, or H Samuel the jeweller's, right, supplied local businessmen with the obligatory gold timepiece and chain for their waistcoat pockets. The New Theatre (left), which burned down a few years later, was replaced in the 1960s with the large Churchill Theatre.

► **CHISLEHURST**
Prickend Pond c1965
C97029

This picturesque small lake, often complete with ducks, sits at the northern end of a common in a large village. Prickend marks the end of one expanse of land that stretches from Petts Wood in the south and to Summer Hill in the west. The pond dates back to at least the 16th century, and is associated with the Manors of Chislehurst, Scadbury and St Paul's Cray. In a hot summer the pond decides to dry up until the autumn rains descend.

SIDCUP
The Green 1900 45817

Straw boaters were de rigeur for these smart Victorian children. Do you think the horse and cart, left, had dropped them off to enjoy a picnic in this picturesque spot? More than a hundred years later little has changed around the Green, and the attractive red brick house seen here remains as attractive as it ever was.

◄ **BEXLEY**
High Street c1955
B83040

Here we have an early morning scene in a busy little village. Nine years after this picture was taken the road and these charming brick cottages would be under the administrative wing of the Greater London Authority. Today the traffic along this stretch is constant as motorists head towards the A2 to reach the capital.

◄ **SIDCUP**
The Oval c1955
S127060

The half-timbered top storeys of all these shops added an attractive architectural extra to this suburban part of the town. Dewhurst the butcher, sixth left, was one of many traders familiar to shoppers in the 1950s. Today this parade of shops sit by a much busier road than the one we see here.

▲ **BEXLEY,** *St Mary's Church c1955* B83008

This church began life in the 12th century, and underwent a major restoration in the 19th century. The tower stands out because of its unique design of an unusual octagonal shingled spire. In 1853 the great-grandparents of Queen Elizabeth II married here.

◄ **ERITH**
High Street c1953
E58014

Queen Elizabeth II visited this town in 1953 to offer her condolences to the hundreds of residents whose lives had been torn apart by a monstrous flood that wrecked homes and businesses. It is interesting to note that the Burton chain of menswear shops, like the one pictured here (right), have recently celebrated fifty years in business.

CRAYFORD
Saint Paulinus's Church c1955 C528006

This Norman church atop Crayford Hill is probably the oldest in the borough of Bexley. The earliest parts of the north nave date from c1100, and another nave and chancel were constructed in the 14th century. The tower dates from the 15th century, and the vestry from the 16th century. A church was recorded as being on this site in the Domesday Book, when a 'ford' was built over the River Cray.

CRAYFORD, *The Riverside c1965* C528015

The town was a regular target for bombing raids during the Second World War because of its close proximity to the Woolwich Arsenal. Crayford was very much a place of industry in the 20th century: it boasted a tannery, the famous Vickers aircraft factory, a silk manufacturer, and Swaizlands Fabric Factory.

NORTH KENT

LEAVING Crayford we soon arrive in Dartford - birthplace of Rolling Stone Sir Mick Jagger and the resting place of the great 18th-century engineer, Richard Trevithick. Just outside the town are the famous toll tunnels passing under the River Thames to and from Essex. At the end of the 20th century, Queen Elizabeth II opened a dramatic new bridge bearing her name across the river. The villages surrounding Dartford include Eynsford and the picturesque Darenth Valley, and at Greenhithe is Europe's largest shopping mall, Bluewater. In Swanscombe a skull belonging to a Neolithic man was discovered in recent years. The small but lively town of Swanley attracts many visitors, and is situated near Lullingstone Castle, home to Tom Hart Dyke, the well known orchid hunter. Along the river is Gravesend, once a busy port with a pier, and the former home of General Gordon of Khartoum. The town has a statue of Pocahontas, the Native American princess, who is believed to be buried there. Her claim to fame is that she saved the life of the 17th-century adventurer Captain Smith, and married John Rolfe, an English settler in Virginia. Nearby Northfleet housed a giant cement works. In the villages and hamlets of Shorne, Cobham, Hartley, Vigo, Harvel and Meopham are farms, pretty cottages, churches and a windmill.

DARTFORD
High Street 1902
49017

This early Edwardian dusty street scene reminds me of a cowboy film! Close scrutiny of this picture shows us a hardware shop (left), Staffordshire House, established in 1849. Next door is Bartlett & Cain the drapers. Across the street is the New Inn, Boots the chemist, and Upson & Co, 'The Great Boot Providers'.

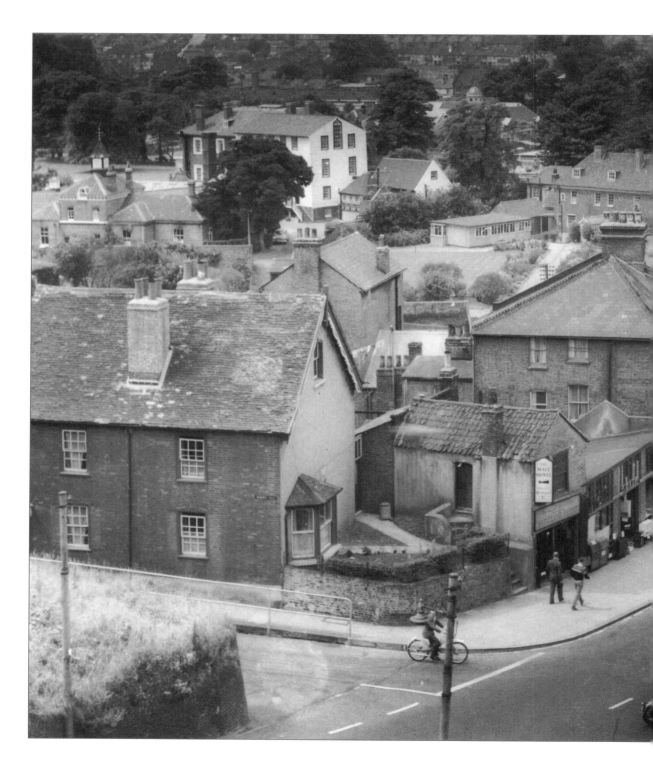

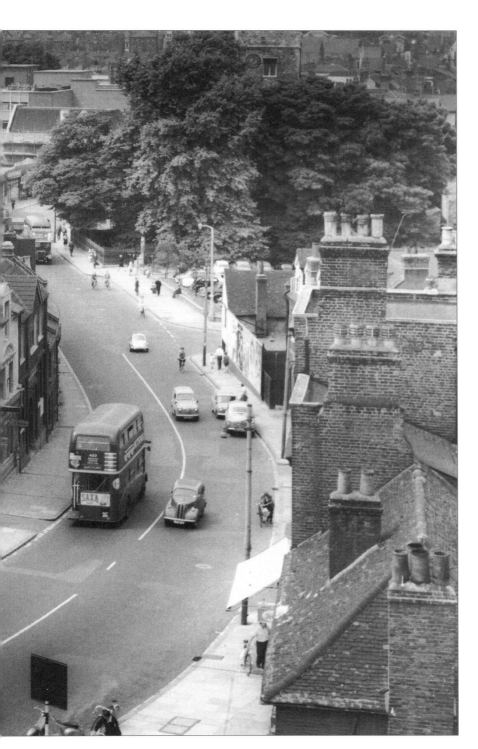

DARTFORD
c1960 D3056

Dartford was home to two
of the world's most famous
rock stars, Sir Mick Jagger
and Keith Richards, and
this is how they would
remember the town of
their youth. On the left is
a pub known as the Malt
Shovel, and the 480 bus has
journeyed to this point from
Temple Hill. In fact, the
same bus probably helped
ferry the future Rolling
Stones to and from band
practice.

▼ **EYNSFORD,** *The Church 1905* 53254

St Martin's Church, with its wood-shingled spire, has a tower clock surrounded by a quotation from the poet Robert Browning - 'Grow old along with me, the best is yet to be.' The western entrance is Norman. The village of Eynsford was once home to a well known man of Kent, the writer and historian Arthur Mee.

► **SWANLEY**
The Village c1950
S389022

This was the year that the Whitbread brewery began making special celebration pub signs. The Red Lion sign, dominating this picture, was a familiar sight to many villagers who enjoyed the pub's selection of local ales. In 1966 the construction of a new A20 by-pass rescued this village from the horrors of becoming a 'rat run'.

◄ **GREENHITHE**
HMS 'Worcester'
c1955 G215001

This floating school set up by the Royal Navy had trained hundreds of ships' crew from all over the world. In 1962 this famous instruction base was visited by Queen Elizabeth II and the Duke of Edinburgh. In more recent years the Royal Navy decided to pull out of the area, which is now dominated by Europe's largest shopping mall, Bluewater.

► **BRANDS HATCH**
c1960 B579023

This scene is a far cry from the sight of today's crowds who now flock to the 2.65 mile circuit to witness the thrills and spills of motor racing. In 1926 it was just an old grass track and mushroom field used by young cyclists. Today the owners are fighting to upgrade the current track to get its Grand Prix status back again.

◄ **WROTHAM**
The Church 1901
47640

St George's Church, chiefly 13th- and 15th-century, boasts an imposing tower with a vaulted passage at its base to allow processions to remain on consecrated land. I wonder if these parishioners were impressed by its memorial brass portrait gallery, with 50 figures of five families dating from 1498 to 1615.

▲ **SEAL CHART,** *The Church 1901* 47620

The church of St Lawrence was built in 1867. It is situated next to the primary school in wooded country on the chart ('la chert' means 'common'). The Reverend Thomas Offspring Blackall, vicar from 1846 to 1874, who created the separate parish of Seal Saint Lawrence, is buried here. A window on the north aisle was installed in his memory.

◄ **BOROUGH GREEN**
Western Road 1903
51023

I would love to know what these children were doing along this quiet residential road. Were the eight boys reluctantly looking after the toddler for a busy mum? And what games were they planning with the two wheelbarrows? Today this road is a busy traffic thoroughfare used by motorists bound for Sevenoaks and/or the M20.

▶ **IGHTHAM**
Ightham Mote
1900 44913

This 14th-century
building with its
15 bedrooms and
ancient halls boasts
a fascinating list of
owners including
knights, MPs, sheriffs
and businessmen.
Mystery surrounded
the old mote when
a skeleton was
discovered bricked
up in a wall. In 1900
the house belonged
to Sir Thomas Colyer-
Ferguson. In 1953
it belonged to an
American, Charles
Henry Robinson, who
bequeathed it to the
National Trust in 1985.

◀ **IDE HILL**
The Church c1960
I49035

The shingled spire of
St Mary the Virgin stands
out among the stunning
views of this small village.
The church was built
in 1807, and aimed at
serving a population of
just under a thousand at
that time. Its architecture
is deemed modern
compared to many other
Kent places of worship
that began life in Norman
times.

▲ **CROCKHAM HILL,** *Holy Trinity Church c1960* C467025

Built in 1842, this striking place of worship sits just a few hundred yards from Chartwell - the former home of the wartime prime minister, Sir Winston Churchill. Over the years the church has attracted many visitors, and forms part of the Diocese of Rochester.

◄ **WESTERHAM**
The George and Dragon c1955 W61020

The most famous resident of this attractive village was Sir Winston Churchill, who lived a short walk away at Chartwell. His local was the white-washed, stone-built George and Dragon, which is as busy today as it was when his picture was taken. The Oxford 'bags' worn by the man outside the white weather-boarded teashop are a fetching sight.

▼ **SEVENOAKS,** *High Street and the Church 1900* 44905

This country town is close to one of the noblest houses in Kent - the Jacobean home of the Sackvilles, Knole. St Nicholas's Church (left) has a 90ft-high tower and turret with a cupola. William Sevenoke, who is described as a foundling discovered in the hollow of a tree 500 years ago, built the grammar school in 1432 and almshouses atop Sevenoaks Hill.

► **OTFORD**
Morris Dancing on the Green c1955 O87035A

Led by the fiddle-player on the right, and probably lubricated by the pub behind him, Morris dancers perform on the village green in the year that ended post-war rationing. Brandishing their handkerchiefs, these dancers are celebrating an ancient custom still alive (and kicking) today. Morris dancers are recorded as greeting Charles II in Kent on his return from exile.

◄ **BRASTED**
High Street c1955
B580020

What wonderful examples of 1950s fashion are being sported by the middle-aged couple, right. Ten years later, the designer Laura Ashley opened a mill in the village to mark the start of what has become a fashion empire still in business throughout Britain today. During the Second World War the White Hart pub was popular with RAF fighter pilots stationed at nearby Biggin Hill.

► **HEVER**
The Village 1906
53550

Around 350 years before this tranquil scene was captured, horses like these would have been ridden around the village by the knights of King Henry VIII. He was a frequent visitor to Hever Castle, the childhood home of his second wife, Anne Boleyn. The spire of the ancient church, left, is tucked behind the site of an inn which has existed since 1597.

▼ **PENSHURST,** *Penshurst Place 1891* 29392

This sprawling 14th-century house is an impressive sight. It was the birthplace of the poet-soldier Sir Philip Sidney, who died for his country in 1582. More than 350 years later his descendant, Major Philip Sidney, was awarded a Victoria Cross for gallantry in the Second World War. Today the house is open to the public.

► **CHIDDINGSTONE**
*The Church and the
School 1891* 29399

Situated next to Penshurst Station, this village grew to accommodate visitors on their way to take goods to the town. The railway was built in 1850, providing easy access to London, Tonbridge and Sevenoaks. The construction of St Mary's Church and its neighbouring primary school followed shortly after. In 1860 the village was home to Duke & Sons, famous makers of cricket bats and balls.

◄ **BENENDEN**
The Village c1960
B570009

With its white weather-boarded houses and leafy glades, this village was once home to Viscount Rothermere. His great-uncle, Alfred Harmsworth, founded the Daily Mail in 1896, and the family lived at the house which was to become the private Benenden School. Famous old girls include Princess Anne and the author Sue Ryder. Did they ever collect their pocket money from the Westminster Bank (right)?

► **KEMSLEY**
The Village c1955
K123004

A very regular row of houses lines this quiet street. I wonder if all the residents were enjoying their first taste of commercial television? This was the year that the BBC found it had a rival on the small screen, and the world of advertising had taken on new impetus.

► **TUNBRIDGE WELLS**
The Pantiles 1885
T87302

Then, just as it is today, this area of the town was an exclusive parade of expensive little shops, smart tea shops and expensive restaurants. Here we see two children standing with a woman outside a shop we can just make out as G Featherstone (left). A printer's and stationer's shop, R Felton, sits next door. Queen Victoria had been known to visit the town during her long reign, which helped sustain its title of Royal Tunbridge Wells.

◄ **BEDGEBURY**
Bedgebury House 1902 48317

The Culpepers built Bedgebury Park in a classical style from the profits of the Wealden iron industry. In 1836 the Napoleonic war hero Viscount Beresford retired here. In 1854 his heir, Alexander Beresford-Hope, cased the house in Wealden sandstone and added another storey in the English Gothic style. Today it is a private school.

▲ **PLAXTOL,** *Rats Castle 1901* 47610

This rambling 15th-century hall house has changed little over the years. It is inscribed with the initials of Stephen Chilman, who modernised it in the 17th century. Today it is a private home.

◄ **TONBRIDGE**
High Street c1950
T101014

Boys on bicycles, shoppers and motorists throng this street, and there is every sign that the public library (left) had a regular flow of readers who still did not have the luxury of owning a newly invented television set. Meanwhile, local schoolboy Michael Colin Cowdrey, 17, made his debut for Kent County Cricket Club in this year.

▼ **HADLOW,** *Post Office Corner 1960* H461020

In this village churchyard there is a 19th-century memorial to thirty hop pickers who drowned when their cart slipped over a crumbling bridge and dragged them into the depths of the River Medway. In 1859 Walter Barton May built a 170ft-tall tower at Hadlow Castle, and in 1951 it became protected by a special preservation order. The tower is very prominent in the mid-Kent landscape.

► **CHIPSTEAD**
The Downs c1960
C463003

Bordering the wonderful weald of Kent, Chipstead is near the great house of Chevening - a favourite spot for Prince Charles. The views in this area, like the view this picture depicts, attract many visitors every year and have been the site of many a great picnic and family day out.

◄ **PADDOCK WOOD**
Hop Picking c1955
P220019

A whole row of hop vines have been pulled to the ground ready for the nimble fingers of these workers to detach the hops and bundle them into bushels ready for transportation to local breweries. This autumn activity was a favourite country job for Londoners keen to escape the city and make some money at the same time.

► **COWDEN**
High Street c1955
C225009

Almost fifty years after this tranquil scene was captured by our photographer, this village near Edenbridge would become known as the place of a dreadful train crash which killed five and injured 11 in 1994. It happened in a thick autumn mist when two trains collided on the single line running through the village station.

► **CRANBROOK**
Stone Street 1906
56971

Weather-boarded and glass shop fronts line this Edwardian street, which boasts a jeweller's, a draper's and silk mercer's named Stokes & Sons, and a trader by the name of J F Gammon. The village windmill sits proudly overlooking the street, while the licensee J Fread at the Prince Albert pub (right) offered 'good stabling' for drinkers' horses.

CRANBROOK
St David's Bridge
1921 70176

The summer of this year is on record as being suffocatingly hot, and this village, like most in Kent, suffered from a completely rainless June and July. Perhaps the man in the cap (left), riding one heavy horse and leading another, is on his way to stock up on water from the local river?

◄ **HORSMONDEN**
The Green 1903 50551

A big part of the old Wealden Ironworks was based here, and a man-made furnace pond was dug. In the 17th century a feisty character named John Browne built cannons here, but the foundry closed in 1685 because of Browne's political allegiances. A pub called the Gun and Spitroast opened in 1750 in memory of those days. It is also home to the 'fuggle' hop.

▼ **LAMBERHURST,** *The Village Bridge and Broadway c1960* L323057

Although deserted when this picture was taken, this attractive village was populated enough to sustain two pubs, the George and Dragon, left, and the Chequers Inn beyond. Nearby is Scotney Castle, owned at this time by one of the Hussey family, historic ironmasters of Kent. By 1975 the future prime minister Margaret Thatcher and her family had moved to a house here known as The Mount.

► **GOUDHURST**
The Village 1901 46377

This scene was snapped from the church and faces down the hill. On the right is the Goudhurst Coffee House, and it looks as if a shop is next door. Eedes the chemist sits behind the trees (centre). I wonder if the horse and cart, left, was on its way to collect the hops recently picked in the fields nearby.

◄ **GOUDHURST**
Measuring the Hops 1904 52571

The newly installed railway connection serving the Weald of Kent had no doubt dropped many of these workers off to start work in the hop fields. They all seem relaxed enough to pose for the camera as they weigh in their bushels for the farmer. A hundred years later, much of their handiwork would be replaced by machines.

► **SISSINGHURST**
The Village 1903
51021

Is the old chap (right) on his way to the Bull Inn for a pint of local ale or cider? If he was still around 27 years later, he no doubt would have met the poet, novelist and gardener Vita Sackville-West and her diplomat husband, Sir Harold Nicolson. The couple had just moved into Sissinghurst Castle in 1930; centuries earlier, the castle had been a prison for foreign soldiers.

45

MAIDSTONE
High Street 1898 41536

What an unusual
combination of goods
the trader is selling in the
third shop from the right:
fishing tackle and fireworks!
Today this large town by
the River Medway looks
very different. It teems with
traffic, and it is the County
Town of Kent. A prison
that has housed some of
Britain's most notorious
criminals is nearby.

LOOSE
The Village 1898
41560

Although many more homes have been built here since this picture was taken, it remains famous for its contribution to hop growing in Kent. Today it is home to the artist Ralph Steadman - and to the incongruously named Loose Women's Institute!

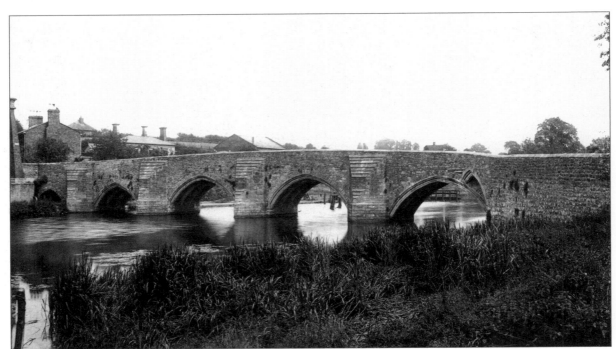

EAST FARLEIGH, *The Bridge 1898* 41558

With its five arches, this ragstone bridge over the River Medway is said to be the finest medieval bridge in the south of England. The first record of it was in 1324, when an official inquiry was held into who was responsible for its upkeep. During the Civil War, in 1648, General Fairfax and the Parliamentary Army crossed the bridge and captured Maidstone from the Royalists.

SUTTON VALENCE, *The Weald c1960* S544024

The wondrous sight of blossom continues to greet many a springtime visitor to this central part of the county, where orchards are a prime feature. The village school's most famous old boy is Sydney Wooderson, a Blackheath Harrier, who in 1937 ran a mile in just four minutes and 6.4 seconds.

▼ **BARMING,** *Blossom Time c1960* B568013

This rural scene of blossom trees is mostly a forgotten sight here today. The village has been eclipsed by 20th-century housing developments. However, there is still a good view from the Norman St Margaret's Church. Reminders of the old village can still be seen, including St Helen's - a wooden bridge now closed to traffic.

▶ **MARDEN**
High Street c1965
M252028

Nestling in the borough of Maidstone, this village is made up of three main streets. Its old courthouse remains in the centre, and the stocks where local criminals met their punishment are now on show in the 13th-century church of St Michael and St Angels. The glass in the chancel windows was designed in 1962 by Patrick Reyntiens.

◀ **YALDING**
The Anchor c1960
Y35019

This aptly named pub sits in a quiet cove in a village often plagued by flooding. The inn has over the years provided shelter to many villagers whose homes have been plundered by the lashings of storms and rising tides. In this picture the still waters of the River Medway run deep.

▶ **ALLINGTON**
The Castle c1955
A230020

Having survived yet another war, this ancient battlement enjoys a total restoration carried out by its owner Sir Martin Conway in 1905. In 1951 it was bought by the Carmelite Order and used as a 'desert house' for its members - here the sisters could spend a year in contemplation before going back to their professional lives. Today, it still attracts many visitors.

AYLESFORD *from the air 1932* AF38096

► **AYLESFORD**
Kit's Coty c1960
A85041

There has been much debate about the age and significance of these four giant stones a mile north of the village. The most popular theory is that Kit's Coty - 'coty' means 'house' - was the burial place of Catigern, who is said to have fallen fighting the legendary Anglo-Saxon warriors Hengist and Horsa in the Battle of Aylesford in AD 455.

◄ **AYLESFORD**
The Bridge c1960
A85046

This is the birthplace of the celebrated 20th-century actress, Dame Sybil Thorndike. Little has changed here over the years, despite the growth of the paper mill. A barrier gate system is now in operation over this busy bridge. The George Hotel, right, and the tobacconist and the teashop pictured nearby shared the village with Kent's smallest pub, the Little Gem.

▶ **CHATHAM**
*The Town Hall
c1955* C69013

Sitting lofty and proud on the road to the famous dockyard, this majestic building, built in 1900, was once the centre of the town's administration until it moved to Strood during an amalgamation of Medway councils. Now it is known as the Brook Theatre. The architect who designed it, G E Bond, also built the Grade II listed Chatham Theatre Royal in Manor Road in 1899.

◀ **ROCHESTER**
*The Castle and the
Cathedral 1894* 34029

This Victorian boatman seems to be having problems managing his sails! There seemed to be a swell on the River Medway that day, but the photographer kept a steady hand to capture the imposing sights of the Norman castle and the cathedral. The city was known as the home of the novelist Charles Dickens, who died in 1870.

► **GADS HILL**
The Residence of Charles Dickens 1894 34045

This extraordinary old manor house had been bereft of its famous author owner, Charles Dickens, for 24 years when this picture was taken. Dickens died here on 9 June 1870 at the age of 58. Today the house and copious grounds are home to a private girls' school. A Swiss chalet where the writer penned his last work, 'The Mystery of Edwin Drood', sits in Rochester High Street.

◄ **CLIFFE**
High Street c1955
C464015

This village, archaeologists believe, is the 'Cloveshoo' of Saxon times - known then as a big town with several ancient councils. Its full name is Cliffe-at-Hoo. The 19th century brought many labourers to Cliffe, who worked on the Strood canal or the cement works. The Victorian Black Bull pub (centre) is now a renowned Thai restaurant. Plans to build an airport here were defeated by angry villagers in 2003.

▲ **ALLHALLOWS,** *The Beach c1955* A229014

This small landing bay off the Thames estuary near the Isle of Grain is popular with fishermen and amateur sailors. The hook, centre foreground, and mooring blocks suggest that a small craft is often tied here, and the bathing huts, right, are well kept and brightly painted. Is the woman on the shingle the owner of what looks like a coat atop the concrete pyramid, right?

◄ **HOO**
Marina Caravan Site
c1960 H356039

At this time, many found it fashionable to have a boat, and decided to buy a moveable home and moor it in Hoo, or to give it its full name, Hoo St Werburgh, the dedication of the church. In the 19th century a brickworks and pottery dominated the scene. Today the local industry is agriculture, but the marina remains popular.

RAINHAM
The Church c1960 R80018

The tower stands tall and proud, and it is not difficult to understand why St Margaret's was one of several beacons forming a connection with other churches from London to the coast. Built in 1488, the tower is constructed of Kentish ragstone; the east wall of the chancel is 11th-century. Parish records are kept in a rare 14th-century chest in the Tufton chapel.

▼ **GILLINGHAM,** *The Entrance to the Strand c1955* G144013

This riverside spot remains as popular today as it did in the 1950s. It sits near to Brompton Barracks, and now forms part of the Black Lion Leisure Centre. I wonder who picked up the litter on the pavement outside the café, right?

► **MILTON REGIS**
High Street c1955
M256016

Before becoming engulfed in the sprawl of Sittingbourne, Milton was a royal manor in its own right. Indeed, it is known as the Middleton of Alfred the Great, and its flint and stone Holy Trinity Church is the second oldest in Kent. A beamed and peg tiled old court house still stands in the main street not far from the White Hart pub, right.

SITTINGBOURNE
High Street c1960
S531037

It is early morning or a summer's evening in this significant mid-Kent town. A good selection of traders line the left side of the street, including W J Dolding & Son and a bakery. Further along is the Golden Eagle pub and Boots the Chemist. The Methodist church, right, makes an austere impression.

TESTON
Orchard Stores Corner c1960 T229019

Many years before D G Sheppard opened his Orchard Stores, an entrepreneur named Alfred Reader had set up his cricket and hockey ball factory in the 1820s. To reach this village one can cross a medieval ragstone bridge across the River Medway. The Vicar of St Peter and St Paul's Church, James Ramsay, played a major part in ensuring the abolition of slavery. He died in 1789.

BREDGAR
The Street c1960
B581003

The church of St John has a beautiful tower, which overlooks this splendid-looking family home. In February 1960 the church bells rang throughout the villages of Kent to herald the birth of Prince Andrew.

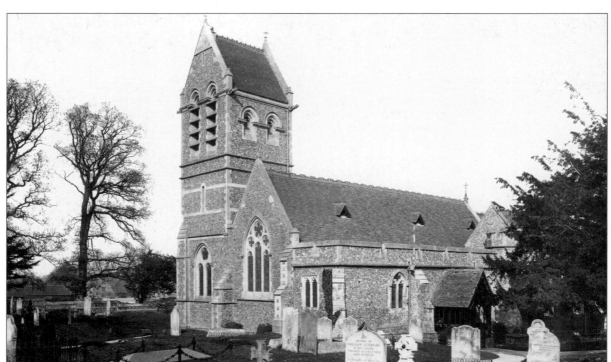

OSPRINGE, *The Church 1892* 31476

In 1695 many had a narrow escape when the bell tower collapsed during an energetic ringing session serenading a visit by William III. The church of St Peter and St Paul is like many churches built in Norman times - it is situated near a spring. This adds 'purity' to the Christian message. In 1866 restoration work saw the completion of the saddleback tower.

LEYSDOWN-ON-SEA, *Station Road c1960* L326032

Leysdown is a popular holiday resort on the Isle of Sheppey, reached by crossing the Kingsferry Bridge. Traders enjoyed brisk business here - they include the busy Choc Box, an amusement arcade, the Cabin Tea Rooms and a beachwear outlet. More than 40 years later, many visitors continue to pour in to stay at a resident caravan park offering karaoke and clubland singers on the entertainment bill.

EASTCHURCH
High Street c1960
E153010

Here on the Isle of Sheppey life does not get much quieter. These buses going to and from Sheerness provided many villagers with their only transport to the main town on the island. The tall poles in the street indicate the advancements in communication technology made that year by the nearby Medway Telephone Exchange.

DETLING, *The Church c1960* D164019

St Martin of Tours' Church is on the main Pilgrims' Way from Winchester to Canterbury, and would have been a regular stopping point for the pilgrims before starting the climb up Detling Hill. The church has traces of its original Norman structure, but most of what can be seen today is Early English.

LEEDS CASTLE
1892 31503

This battlemented castle has always been heralded for its beauty. It had been a Norman stronghold and a royal residence. In the 19th century much reconstruction had taken place. By 1926 its owner, the Honourable Mrs Wilson-Fulmer (Lady Baillie) had begun a 30 year restoration project. Today it is hailed as 'the loveliest castle in the world', and plays host to regular star-studded classical concerts.

LENHAM, *Faversham Road c1960* L322004

Evidence that this village existed in Roman times was unearthed just after the Second World War. Workmen in the Square found the skeletons of two men and a woman; both men had been buried with a sword and shield. Archaeologists believed that they were early Christians. Today, the village and its Tudor buildings is one of Kent's largest and busiest on the A20 road to Maidstone and Ashford.

FAVERSHAM, *West Street 1892* 31470

Home to Britain's oldest brewery, Shepherd Neame, this town sits near many fruit trees and hop fields. The crowd in this picture look as if they are waiting for the trader on the corner to open his doors for business. The open windows above them set in a bay against a brick frontage suggest it is a warm day.

EAST AND SOUTH KENT

HEAD towards Faversham, home to Britain's oldest brewery, and very soon the breathtaking sight of Canterbury's celebrated cathedral hits the skyline. The city, one of the most visited in the world, is the origin of Geoffrey Chaucer's famous 'Canterbury Tales', and the birthplace of the 16th-century playwright Christopher Marlowe. Taking in the villages on the way to the coastal towns of Dover, Deal, Folkestone, Hythe, Dymchurch, and Romney Marsh, we reach Bridge, Bishopsbourne and Broome Park - a stately home owned by Lord Kitchener, who enjoyed a fine view of the Barham Downs. A few miles on from Canterbury, we reach Whitstable and its famous oyster houses; then we come to Herne Bay, Margate, Ramsgate and Minster. The A28 from the cathedral city leads to the former market town of Ashford, whose villages (including Hothfield, Westwell, Charing, Chilham, Wye and Pluckley) are surrounded by acres of rolling Kent countryside. Continue on this main road to pass through Bethersden and reach the little old-fashioned town of Tenterden. Just outside here is Smallhythe, one of the last villages in Kent before we get into East Sussex. It was at Smallhythe that the great Victorian actress Dame Ellen Terry lived. Her home is now a National Trust property.

BOUGHTON
The Village c1965
B575029

Many fine old buildings
line this long street,
which was a pilgrims'
route into Canterbury.
St Barnabas's Church
stands behind the two
gate pillars (right), and
a memorial in a nearby
wall lists the village's
fallen from the First
and Second World Wars.
Today little has changed
in this scenic spot.

CANTERBURY, *The Cathedral 1888* 21357

This magnificent cathedral heralds the beginning of English Christianity: Augustine was appointed its first archbishop in 597. Over the centuries it has been witness to fire and murder. In 1170 its then archbishop, Thomas a Becket, was slaughtered there by four knights of Henry II. By the late 19th century the Pilgrims' Way through London to Kent had brought many visitors to its doors.

CANTERBURY, *The Cathedral, Bell Harry Tower 1890* 25674

This Victorian snapshot of what is arguably the country's most famous landmark gives us a westerly view of the spectacular Bell Harry Tower. Most parts of the building seen here would have been familiar to the medieval writer, Geoffrey Chaucer - author of 'The Canterbury Tales'.

▶ **CANTERBURY**
*St Dunstan's
Street c1955*
C18047

This street in a
medieval and famous
city is serenaded
by the majestic
Westgate Towers. New
in Chaucer's time,
they were built by
Archbishop Sudbury
and replaced a ruin
on the same spot.
Visitors stayed, and
still do, at the
Falstaff Hotel (left,
established in 1403),
and bought bread
from neighbouring
Hopper's the bakers.
A pub known as the
Gun can be seen
opposite.

BRIDGE
From the Mill 1903
49398

What a tranquil sight
greeted the miller every
morning a hundred years
ago. The dominant feature
is the Norman St Peter's
Church presiding over this
view. In 1853 the church
had been restored in
Kentish flint. An unusual
sculpture of its 16th-
century priest, Macobus
Kasey, still attracts many
visitors to this busy village
which has three pubs, a
butcher, a baker, a school
and a health centre.

▲ **BRIDGE,** *Bifrons 1903* 49409

This magnificent stone mansion was the new home of the racing driver Count Louis Zborowski; with Captain John Howey, he created the famous Romney, Hythe & Dymchurch Railway. The Count also raced the Chitty Chitty Bang Bang car, the subject of a Disney film. Bifrons was the former seat of the Marquess of Conyngham.

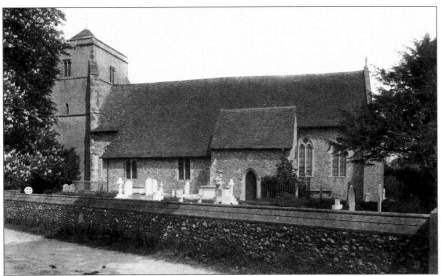

◄ **BISHOPSBOURNE**
The Church 1903 49417

With its Norman doorway, medieval wall paintings and 17th-century Flemish glass window, St Mary's Church sits in an idyllic rural setting. Its most famous rector was the 16th-century theologian Richard Hooker, who wrote 'The Laws of Ecclesiastical Polity'. He died in 1600 and is buried in the graveyard. Beside the graveyard is Oswalds, once home to the novelist Joseph Conrad.

FORDWICH, *The River c1960* F38008

Just as they do today, the boys who lived in this historic town - Fordwich is the smallest town in Britain - enjoyed boating on the River Stour which ebbed and flowed between Canterbury and the sea. During the Second World War, the Kent-born film director Michael Powell and his Archers production company featured the town and its oak beamed houses in his famous propaganda epic, 'A Canterbury Tale'.

FORDWICH, *The Town Hall and the Dipping Chair 1898* 40854

Built during the reign of Henry VIII, this tiny town hall is now a listed building. It was also a courtroom and prison. On the ground floor, we see the room where the jury was sent to consider its verdict. Above is a dipping chair, which was used to duck women in the river for being a 'scold' or a gossip.

▼ **WICKHAMBREUX,** *The Post Office 1903* 51048

The stores and post office, right, were once an essential part of this village. Today, the property is called The Old Stone House, and all that remains of its Royal Mail connections are a pillar box set in a wall and a telephone box. The bridge, left, crossed the Lesser Stour River. Further left is an old water mill once used by a large farming community.

► **NONINGTON**
The Church c1955
N142029

Little has changed in this quiet spot, with St Mary's Church still attracting a fair amount of visitors to see its Early English features. In the chancel is the Hammond family vault. The last of this well-known village family, Douglas William, died in the First World War aged just 18. Two war memorials stand in the churchyard.

◀ **LITTLEBOURNE**
The Square 1903
51052

Are the village women, right, considering a visit to the Anchor pub for a glass of cider? Perhaps they had already imbibed at the King William IV inn, a drinking house dating back to 1790 at the east side of the Square. Looking after children can be thirsty work.

▶ **WHITSTABLE**
Marine Terrace 1950
W405016

The Old Neptune pub (centre left) has not changed much since the photographer snapped this picture. However, the houses on the right would not fare so well three years later when high winds hit the coast, rendering the new sea wall completely inadequate. This coastal town, famed for its oysters, was one of many to suffer in the great tides of 1953, which damaged many homes and businesses.

► **HERNE BAY**
From the Pier
1897 40150

Promenading in the afternoon, these late Victorians are out to see - and to be seen. A group of London businessmen founded the town in 1837. Hotels such as the Dolphin, right, did brisk business as the resort established a reputation for peace and quiet, plentiful sunshine and fresh, clean air, which was said to arrive untainted from the Arctic Circle.

◄ **HERNE BAY**
The Esplanade 1897
40158

The esplanade with its wide pavements proved an excellent place for exercise and recreation - goat carts (like the one on the left) were a common amusement at seaside resorts. During the Second World War the scientist Barnes Wallis experimented with his famous bouncing bomb along this stretch of the Channel.

▲ **BROADSTAIRS,** *The Harbour 1897* 39591

In Queen Victoria's reign it was not 'proper' to enter the sea without a bathing machine. Once wheeled out to a suitable depth, these examples, right, enabled the bather to maintain his or her modesty while plunging in! This busy fishing resort was also a favourite of Charles Dickens; he found the sea air inspired him to complete his novel 'Nicholas Nickleby' here.

◄ **BROADSTAIRS**
The Promenade 1902
48842

Sporting the new Edwardian fashions of ankle-length skirts and more liberal corsetry, these promenaders are enjoying the sea breeze. It is ironic that the toy steam engine on wheels ridden by the toddler, right, would soon be upstaged by models of electric trams - a mode of transport unveiled by King Edward VII in this year

BROADSTAIRS
Broadstairs Sands 1912
65021

What a typically English
seaside scene. The child on
the right enjoys a donkey
ride, while her friends on
the left dig deep in the sand.
I bet the tough sailor suit
sported by the boy nearby
keeps out the sea breezes.

BROADSTAIRS, *York Gate c1960* B220024

This unusual monument was built in 1538 by George Culmer in a bid to protect the shipyard in nearby Harbour Street. Originally it was called the Flint Gate; then it was re-named after the Grand Old Duke of York and re-built in 1795 by Lord Henniker. The teashop on the left (supplying trays for the beach) was one of the many refreshment places in this historic little town - a favourite haunt of Charles Dickens.

MINSTER-IN-THANET
The Square c1955
M86019

A good strong 'Maid of Kent' carries her shopping home, right, while the pedestrians, left, look as if they would rather wait for the bus! They may, of course, be waiting for the New Inn (centre) to open its doors and provide them with the chance to discuss how the coastal area was rapidly turning into a prime tourist spot.

ST NICHOLAS-AT-WADE, *The Village c1965* S699028

This village was so called because from here it was easy to wade across the Wantsum, the stretch of sea that created the Isle of Thanet. The village has many Dutch-gabled properties, and its church retains some remarkable 17th-century features. In 1983, workmen digging near this place of worship found a historic burial area in its foundations.

▼ **CLIFTONVILLE,** *The Bungalow Tea Rooms 1918* 68437

There is nothing like some brisk sea air to put a spring in the step. A sign in the window of the unusual-looking tea rooms says:
'£2 Reward. Lost! Gold Brooch'. Perhaps the man with his back to us is on his way to stake his claim. I love the dapper white shoes worn by the man reading the newspaper.

▲ **RAMSGATE,** *The Parade and New Road 1901* 48028

Look at the crowds thronging this seaport in the year that the Thanet Electric Tramways & Lighting Company launched a new service between Margate, Ramsgate, and Broadstairs. A horse-drawn bus from Minster, bottom centre, remained busy, though, and Brockmans Restaurant, fourth building on the right, attracted a hungry crowd.

◄ **WESTGATE-ON-SEA**
St Mildred's Bay, looking West 1918 68421

It may be a few months before the end of the First World War but these families are enjoying a trip to the seaside. The boy in the foreground is wearing the fashionable sailor suit of the day. I hope the woman in the deckchair, right, was not so fast asleep that she get caught out by the tide!

85

RAMSGATE *from the air 1931* AF35453

ST MARGARET'S BAY
The Undercliff 1918
68493

Dressed in their
Edwardian finery, are
these strollers off to
church? The windows of
the grand red brick and
tiled houses are wide
open, which suggests that
a welcome cool breeze is
coming in off the sea. The
chalk cliffs are part of the
White Cliffs of Dover. In
the 1930s, St Margaret's
most famous resident was
the playwright and actor
Sir Noel Coward.

▼ **BISHOPSTONE,** *The Approach to the Village c1960* B573010

This peaceful lane is often used by those keen to watch the boats go by. Many hikers have strolled into this pretty village to see its cliffs and cottages. It is also a haven for birdwatchers, who over the years have recorded rare sightings of the dusky warbler and desert wheatear in Stuart Lane and Chambers Wall.

▶ **DOVER**
Admiralty Pier 1906
56942

This was a year that saw another important step in establishing Dover as one of the world's busiest ports. In 1906, plans for Admiralty Pier were amended to allow the building of a station for the South Eastern & Chatham Railway. Two years earlier, transatlantic liners had begun to use the port.

◄ **DOVER**
Dover Castle 1890
25703

Standing majestically atop the White Cliffs, this fortress is known as the 'guardian of the gateway to England'. It was an important Iron Age site, and the Anglo-Saxons built the original structure. The hill, or motte, beneath was of Norman origin, and Henry III used the castle as a garrison. Its underground tunnel network played an essential part in the Second World War.

► **EYTHORNE**
The Colliery c1960
E158001

This is one of a cluster of collieries which opened in east Kent just before the First World War. Villagers also found work at nearby Snowdown and Tilmanstone. By the 1980s the Conservative government had closed Britain's coal mining industry following a series of crippling strikes. At this time, an air of despondency following mass redundancies swept over many village mining communities.

▶ **DEAL**
The Gardens
c1960 D15090

A glorious array of colour greeted visitors to this part of the town, which had something for everyone. At the time it was home to the Carry On film star Charles Hawtry, who no doubt visited the Corner Parlour (left) for a cup of tea or coffee. Next door is the Beachbrook Hotel and a fishing tackle shop. A long pier off to the right offered amusements and a superb place to fish.

◀ **DEAL**
Victoria Road 1906
56920

It has not been long since a horse or two trotted along this Edwardian street, as the evidence in the centre of the road reveals. A year later many residents would be discussing the horrors of a whirlwind, which ripped through the town wrecking roofs and farms. In 1995 members of the Royal Marine Band died here when the IRA bombed them during a parade.

▲ **KINGSDOWN** *1906* 56925

Kingsdown was a fishing village, with a strong tradition of commitment to the sea from generations of the same families. Some properties remain on the sites once lived in by their Viking forebears. Kingsdown was first known as Romny Codde, and was established around 1200. St John's Church was built by a nobleman, William Curling, in 1850, and a school, now the village hall, was built in 1840.

◄ **WALMER**
The Strand and the Promenade 1924 76078

Peace reigns along the seafront, where E Atkins, a house decorator, has his premises on the left with Mercer & Son, boot makers and repairers, next door. Further along this stretch is the Strand Stores with its large canopy, along with Harris's greengrocer's shop nearby. The old de-activated gun in the foreground adds to the history of this Cinque Port town and its castle - a favourite haunt of the old Queen Mother.

◄ **WOOTTON**
The Church 1890
27397

St Martin's is just off the Dover Road from Canterbury, and has a 13th-century flint tower surrounded by trees. There is an ancient yew at the church gate which must have been growing when Sir Francis Drake was sailing around the world. Under a stone in the chancel is the body of John Saintpyere, who was rector here before the Armada came.

◄ **EASTRY**
*Sandwich Lane
c1960* E154005

Eastry was home
to many miners
who worked down
the east Kent pits.
The mother of
the actress Susan
Hampshire once
lived here too.
Susan, meanwhile,
has always
loved the area,
and moved to a
Georgian house
in nearby historic
Sandwich.

▲ **ASH,** *Moat Farm and Oast Houses c1955* A232006

Who can fault this lovely view of typical rural Kent? Oast houses like these can be seen in the
east and middle of the county; they were used for storing hops, which were dried before being
despatched to the local brewery. The windmill grinding corn provided an essential part of
agricultural life - an example is just visible in the background.

◄ **SANDWICH**
The Barbican 1924
76226

In 1924, this compact
little town had (and
still has) its own town
council. Many of its
buildings are influenced
by 17th-century Dutch
architecture, including
the bridge, which was
passed under by many
boatmen using the canal.
Just upstream is the
Roman site, Richborough
Castle. The town is home
to the famous
St George's Golf Club.

▶ **ELHAM,** *The Village*
c1960 E156010

These half-timbered
houses and stone cottages
are surrounded by the
wonderfully scenic North
Downs. By the time this
picture was taken, many
visitors would have seen the
village's ragstone and flint
church, Tudor properties
and three inns - one of
which dates back to the
17th century. The Elham
Valley Railway line, which
transported many miners
to local pits, opened in 1887
and closed in 1943.

◀ **BARFRESTON**
The Church c1960
B591004

The amazing stone
carvings at the church
of St Nicholas makes this
church one of the most
perfect specimens of
pure Saxon in the country.
All the carvings depict
medieval life, and the bell
is attached to a yew tree
in the churchyard.

◀ **FOLKESTONE**
The Leas and the Bandstand 1897 39554

These strollers adhered to the proper dress code asked of all Victorians who wished to stretch their legs here. At the Grand Hotel nearby, Edward VII was often to be seen enjoying a game of cards and smoking a cigar while wearing what became known as a 'monkey' suit. In 1903 it was the scene of a welcome home party for soldiers who took part in the Boer War.

▼ **FOLKESTONE,** *The Harbour, the Boulogne Boat Leaving 1906* 53474

Towards the end of the 19th century, Folkestone had established itself as a thriving cross-Channel port. The boat in the picture was no doubt carrying many Edwardian passengers on their first trip to Boulogne in Nord Pas de Calais - a mere twenty miles away.

► **FOLKESTONE**
The Beach 1901 48056

Oh, we do like to be beside the seaside! These sunseekers are thoroughly enjoying a paddle in the Channel. A row of small fishing boats is drawn up on the beach; they were used to gather shrimps and lobsters. A lifeboat station (left background) was at the ready to cope with any rescue missions at sea. A large bathing machine can also been seen here (right background).

◄ **CHERITON**
High Street 1903
50389

This was the time of the end of the Boer War, and the man with the bicycle may well have been discussing the subject with the dog owner, right. This shopping parade still exists, but Cobley the milliner and outfitter, Gilbert the baker and the bicycle shop have been replaced with more modern outlets.

▶ **SANDGATE**
High Street 1903
50370

In the year King Edward VII cut a ribbon to launch London's first electric trams, this small town by the sea still used horses to pull its passenger-laden vehicles. Many of the buildings here have exotic French-style balconies and porches. Homes backing directly onto the beach have suffered in recent years from flooding. The Carry On film star Hattie Jacques was born here.

99

► **HYTHE**
The Parade 1918
68149

'I am old enough to walk on my own now!' says the child standing by her pushchair. This stretch of the town was close to a garrison which closed in the middle of the 20th century, but Shorncliffe Barracks remain in nearby Folkestone. Today Hythe stages a popular summer Venetian Festival to celebrate its famous canal, which remains an ideal place for a punt and a day on the water.

◄ **HYTHE**
High Street 1899
44785

Shoppers calling into J Coomber the butcher (second on the right) had to rely on their bicycles to transport their goods home. They would have to wait a year before a motor bus service between Hythe and Cheriton was on the road. Today this little street remains charmingly old-fashioned, with bookshops and a millinery which makes hats for Ladies' Day at Ascot.

▲ **SALTWOOD,** *The Castle 1890* 25895

Here sits a fortress dating back to Roman times. In 1170 the four knights who murdered Thomas à Becket in Canterbury Cathedral gathered here before carrying out their deadly deed. At the end of the 19th century it was in the hands of the Deedes family. Seventy years later, the art historian Kenneth Clark lived here, to be succeeded by his colourful son Alan, the Tory MP.

◄ **BILSINGTON**
The Church c1920
B95301

This little church, dedicated to St Peter and St Paul, sits on the edge of Romney Marshes; its origins go back to the 12th century. A local family famed for its smuggling activities, the Ransleys, are recorded to have been baptised here. The chancel was built in the 13th century.

DYMCHURCH
The Sands 1927 80401

There is never a shortage of children to enjoy the sandy delights of Dymchurch beach. This fashionable holiday destination was home at this time to the Great War artist Paul Nash. Russell Thorndike, brother of the actress Dame Sybil Thorndike, lived here when he wrote the eerie Dr Syn novels set in Romney Marsh. A Martello tower built to keep the French at bay during the Napoleonic wars still stands here.

▲ **DUNGENESS,** *The Lighthouse c1960* D165009
▶ **DUNGENESS,** *The Lighthouse c1965* D165014

In 1600 the southernmost point of Kent with its enormous flat
expanses of shingle and sand proved so treacherous to sailors
that the need for a lighthouse was urgent. By 1635 a coal fire
had been built on this spot, but in 1792 a proper lighthouse was
constructed. This was replaced with a 'new' one in 1904 - the
one pictured in D165009. By 1965 a second lighthouse, pictured
in D165014 was built; it was 140 feet tall, with an automatic light
whose beams could be seen almost 30 sea miles away.

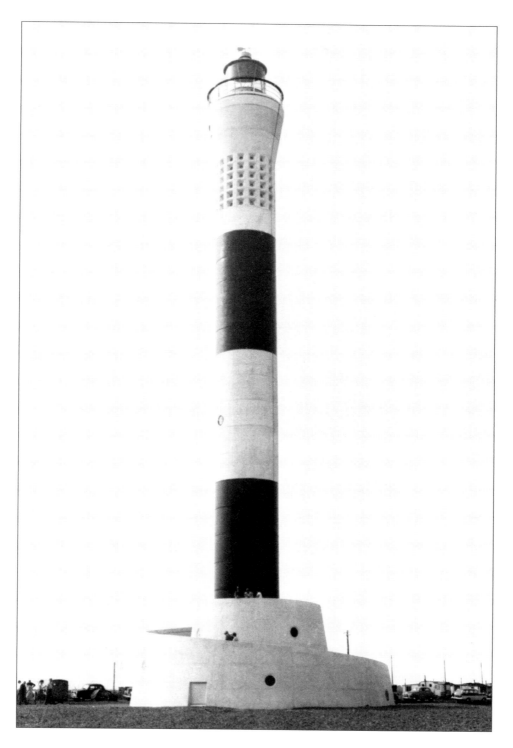

▼ HAM STREET, *The Post Office c1960* H505011

More road signs and traffic markings have since been installed along this stretch of the village. The post office sat right in the corner of the crossroads, where a signpost directed motorists to the marshes, Woodchurch or Ashford. Today this village has several new housing developments. The 19th-century school is a popular choice with local families.

► TENTERDEN
High Street 1900 44990

This was the year that Coca Cola arrived in Kent and an outbreak of typhoid fever terrified local families. At this time the Headcorn to Tenterden railway line was opened. The nearby village of Smallhythe was home to the great Victorian actress, Dame Ellen Terry. A small canal runs through the back of the town on its way to the River Stour. Little in this picture has changed today.

◀ **BIDDENDEN**
The Village c1960
B88004

Home to Kentish cider and several vineyards, this village quite rightly had a thriving wine merchant's, left. Is the man outside deciding whether to opt for a bottle of spirits or local brew? Further along the road is a busy pub, the Red Lion. Today, Biddenden cider can be enjoyed in most Kent pubs.

▶ **HAWKHURST**
Highgate and the Post Office 1925 77043

A costumer and milliner, H H Connolly (third left) ensured that villagers had a chance to sport the latest twenties fashions. The weather-boarded property, left, was a post office, with G H Moorhouse the chemist and a trader, A J Gray, nearby. Are the two men (centre left) discussing the latest scandal of the day - a dance craze known as the Charleston?

▶ **ASHFORD**
Marsh Street 1903
50330

What a shame that this street no longer exists. Today it is called Station Road, and its historic buildings, right, have given way to an office block and a ring road. Only the grandiose Baptist Church remains. The barber's pole which can just be made out on the left indicated a men's hairdressers.

◄ **ROLVENDEN**
The Village and the Church 1901
46451

Many villagers left their homes here between 1830 and 1850 when the parish gave them money to go to Australia. This often meant that they would never return and see scenes like the one pictured here - the 13th-century church of St Mary and all the history that goes with it. The church's most famous vicar was John Frankish, one of the martyrs of 1555 burned at the stake in Canterbury.

► **ASHFORD**
High Street c1950
A71007

Despite the fact that post-war rationing was still in force, this market town was thriving. On the left is an optician's, A Bateman's. Next door, behind the clock, are the Ashford Co-op Society stores, with the Westminster Bank beyond. The white building (centre right) is Alfred Olby, a builders' merchant's. A snack bar, another trader, Jenners, and a wine merchant's are on the right.

ASHFORD, *Middle Row 1908* 60323

Can you spot the white-bearded man peering out at the photographer from the doors of the Man of Kent pub, right? Today this scene has changed very little, although Austin the gunsmith's (left), and the pastrycook's shop (centre) have changed hands many times over the years. The pub, however, remains a popular haunt with the youth of the 21st century.

WILLESBOROUGH
The Lees 1909 61559

Included in this view
(taken from the top of
what is known as the
Broomfields) is the old
Willesborough Hospital.
The year this picture was
taken a cruel winter was
about to strike, leaving
many new owners of
a motor car relying on
horses to pull them free
from snow-laden roads.

WYE, *Bridge Street 1918* 68414

Note the heavily laden horse and cart outside the garage (centre). Like the inhabitants of many villages at the time, the
people here were recovering from the devastating effects of the First World War. Wye sits beneath the chalk hills of the North
Downs; it has a 12th-century church, beautiful Georgian buildings and a college founded in the 1400s by
the Archbishop of Canterbury.

▼ **CHARTHAM,** *The Church and the Green 1903* 50354

St Mary's Church by the charming village green is home to a famous brass dating back to 1306 of Robert de Setvans portraying a military knight. This church was built in 1294, and its tower was constructed in the 15th century. Its windows are fine examples of Kentish tracery. Five of its six bells were made by Joseph Hatch.

► **CHILHAM**
The Square 1913 65334

These half-timbered houses, overlooked by the 15th-century church of St Mary the Virgin, were once homes for local tradesmen from the Jacobean Chilham Castle estate. When this picture was taken, the motor car was a relatively new method of travelling up the hill to the village grocery store, A E Hammond (right). Some visitors, however, still preferred to travel by traditional horse and cart.

◄ **CHARING**
From the Station
1901 47575

A horse and cart waits patiently behind the fence, left. Perhaps it will carry a passenger who had just arrived off one of the steam trains to pass through this attractive village on its way to Ashford. At this time the church bells would have rung in honour of Queen Victoria, who died this year at the age of 81.

► **EASTWELL**
The Towers c1960
E164071

Queen Victoria's second son, the Duke of Edinburgh, had these amazing portico towers built around 1878. Along with the gatehouse next door, they announce the entrance to Eastwell Manor. By 1960 more than 30 years had passed since the house had been given a Jacobean-style facelift. The bastard son of Richard III is buried at the ancient village church.

▶ **WESTWELL**
The Wheel Inn
c1960 W404003

The popular singing duo the Everly Brothers were topping the charts in 1960. Would they be on the jukebox in this historic Kent alehouse? It is only the classic cars that indicate the date of this picture, as today the pub and its surrounding buildings have changed little over the years.

◀ **EGERTON**
The Street c1960
E155010

Was everyone in church or still asleep here? If so, L L Hopkins the grocer and postmaster had managed to get up and open for business! At this time H E Bates - author of 'The Darling Buds of May' - lived in nearby Little Chart Forstal.

▲ **BRABOURNE LEES,** *The Village c1955* B578004

This was the tranquil scene that would have greeted young Queen Elizabeth II and her husband, Prince Philip, when they visited their friends Lord and Lady Brabourne at nearby Mersham. Lady Patricia Brabourne is the daughter of Earl Mountbatten, the cousin of George VI.

◄ **GREAT CHART**
Swinford Manor 1901
47565

Situated two and a half miles from Ashford church, Swinford takes its name from a ford for swine. The manor house dates back to the 13th century, and formed part of a large estate. Its most famous resident was the poet Alfred Austin, who was Poet Laureate from 1896 to 1913. His most well known work is 'The Garden That I Love'. Critics, however, described him as 'snobbish and tasteless'.

HOTHFIELD
On the Common
1921 70317

A violently hot summer was recorded for this year, and this open space with its bracken and ferns was subjected to fires. A blistering heat wave might explain why there is only one motorist brave enough to venture out. Many villagers sought out the cool of the local school (centre) or the medieval church, which sits a mile from the common.

PLUCKLEY, *The Church 1901* 47568

The 13th-century church of St Nicholas is one of several of its kind presiding over the villages of east Kent. It is situated in Britain's most haunted village, and the 'lady in white' has been seen at midnight throwing herself from the bell tower. Nearby is the 15th-century Black Horse Inn. For centuries the land here belonged to the Dering family, whose properties have unusual round-topped windows.

INDEX

The Francis Frith Collection Titles

www.francisfrith.com

The Francis Frith Collection publishes over 100 new titles each year. A selection of those currently available is listed below. For latest catalogue please contact The Francis Frith Collection. **Town Books** 96 pages, approximately 75 photos. **County and Themed Books** 128 pages, approximately 135 photos (unless specified). Pocket Albums are miniature editions of Frith local history books 128 pages, approximately 95 photos.

Accrington Old and New
Alderley Edge and Wilmslow
Amersham, Chesham and Rickmansworth
Andover
Around Abergavenny
Around Alton
Aylesbury
Barnstaple
Bedford
Bedfordshire
Berkshire Living Memories
Berkshire Pocket Album
Blackpool Pocket Album
Bognor Regis
Bournemouth
Bradford
Bridgend
Bridport
Brighton and Hove
Bristol
Buckinghamshire
Calne Living Memories
Camberley Pocket Album
Canterbury Cathedral
Cardiff Old and New
Chatham and the Medway Towns
Chelmsford
Chepstow Then and Now
Cheshire
Cheshire Living Memories
Chester
Chesterfield
Chigwell
Christchurch
Churches of East Cornwall
Clevedon
Clitheroe
Corby Living Memories
Cornish Coast
Cornwall Living Memories
Cotswold Living Memories
Cotswold Pocket Album
Coulsdon, Chipstead and Woodmansterne
County Durham
Cromer, Sheringham and Holt
Dartmoor Pocket Album
Derby
Derbyshire
Derbyshire Living Memories
Devon
Devon Churches
Dorchester

Dorset Coast Pocket Album
Dorset Living Memories
Dorset Villages
Down the Dart
Down the Severn
Down the Thames
Dunmow, Thaxted and Finchingfield
Durham
East Anglia Pocket Album
East Devon
East Grinstead
Edinburgh
Ely and The Fens
Essex Pocket Album
Essex Second Selection
Essex: The London Boroughs
Exeter
Exmoor
Falmouth
Farnborough, Fleet and Aldershot
Folkestone
Frome
Furness and Cartmel Peninsulas
Glamorgan
Glasgow
Glastonbury
Gloucester
Gloucestershire
Greater Manchester
Guildford
Hailsham
Hampshire
Harrogate
Hastings and Bexhill
Haywards Heath Living Memories
Heads of the Valleys
Heart of Lancashire Pocket Album
Helston
Herefordshire
Horsham
Humberside Pocket Album
Huntingdon, St Neots and St Ives
Hythe, Romney Marsh and Ashford
Ilfracombe
Ipswich Pocket Album
Isle of Wight
Isle of Wight Living Memories
King's Lynn
Kingston upon Thames
Lake District Pocket Album
Lancashire Living Memories
Lancashire Villages

Available from your local bookshop or from the publisher

The Francis Frith Collection Titles (continued)

Lancaster, Morecambe and Heysham Pocket Album
Leeds Pocket Album
Leicester
Leicestershire
Lincolnshire Living Memoires
Lincolnshire Pocket Album
Liverpool and Merseyside
London Pocket Album
Ludlow
Maidenhead
Maidstone
Malmesbury
Manchester Pocket Album
Marlborough
Matlock
Merseyside Living Memories
Nantwich and Crewe
New Forest
Newbury Living Memories
Newquay to St Ives
North Devon Living Memories
North London
North Wales
North Yorkshire
Northamptonshire
Northumberland
Northwich
Nottingham
Nottinghamshire Pocket Album
Oakham
Odiham Then and Now
Oxford Pocket Album
Oxfordshire
Padstow
Pembrokeshire
Penzance
Petersfield Then and Now
Plymouth
Poole and Sandbanks
Preston Pocket Album
Ramsgate Old and New
Reading Pocket Album
Redditch Living Memories
Redhill to Reigate
Richmond
Ringwood
Rochdale
Romford Pocket Album
Salisbury Pocket Album
Scotland
Scottish Castles
Sevenoaks and Tonbridge
Sheffield and South Yorkshire Pocket Album
Shropshire
Somerset
South Devon Coast
South Devon Living Memories
South East London
Southampton Pocket Album
Southend Pocket Album
Southport

Southwold to Aldeburgh
Stourbridge Living Memories
Stratford upon Avon
Stroud
Suffolk
Suffolk Pocket Album
Surrey Living Memories
Sussex
Sutton
Swanage and Purbeck
Swansea Pocket Album
Swindon Living Memories
Taunton
Teignmouth
Tenby and Saundersfoot
Tiverton
Torbay
Truro
Uppingham
Villages of Kent
Villages of Surrey
Villages of Sussex Pocket Album
Wakefield and the Five Towns Living Memories
Warrington
Warwick
Warwickshire Pocket Album
Wellingborough Living Memories
Wells
Welsh Castles
West Midlands Pocket Album
West Wiltshire Towns
West Yorkshire
Weston-super-Mare
Weymouth
Widnes and Runcorn
Wiltshire Churches
Wiltshire Living Memories
Wiltshire Pocket Album
Wimborne
Winchester Pocket Album
Windermere
Windsor
Wirral
Wokingham and Bracknell
Woodbridge
Worcester
Worcestershire
Worcestershire Living Memories
Wyre Forest
York Pocket Album
Yorkshire
Yorkshire Coastal Memories
Yorkshire Dales
Yorkshire Revisited

See Frith books on the internet at www.francisfrith.com

FRITH PRODUCTS & SERVICES

Francis Frith would doubtless be pleased to know that the pioneering publishing venture he started in 1860 still continues today. Over a hundred and forty years later, The Francis Frith Collection continues in the same innovative tradition and is now one of the foremost publishers of vintage photographs in the world. Some of the current activities include:

Interior Decoration

Today Frith's photographs can be seen framed and as giant wall murals in thousands of pubs, restaurants, hotels, banks, retail stores and other public buildings throughout the country. In every case they enhance the unique local atmosphere of the places they depict and provide reminders of gentler days in an increasingly busy and frenetic world.

Product Promotions

Frith products are used by many major companies to promote the sales of their own products or to reinforce their own history and heritage. Frith promotions have been used by Hovis bread, Courage beers, Scots Porage Oats, Colman's mustard, Cadbury's foods, Mellow Birds coffee, Dunhill pipe tobacco, Guinness, and Bulmer's Cider.

Genealogy and Family History

As the interest in family history and roots grows world-wide, more and more people are turning to Frith's photographs of Great Britain for images of the towns, villages and streets where their ancestors lived; and, of course, photographs of the churches and chapels where their ancestors were christened, married and buried are an essential part of every genealogy tree and family album.

Frith Products

All Frith photographs are available Framed or just as Mounted Prints and Posters (size 23 x 16 inches). These may be ordered from the address below. From time to time other products - Address Books, Calendars, Table Mats, etc - are available.

The Internet

Already ninety thousand Frith photographs can be viewed and purchased on the internet through the Frith websites and a myriad of partner sites.

For more detailed information on Frith companies and products, look at this site:

www.francisfrith.com

See the complete list of Frith Books at:

www.francisfrith.com

This web site is regularly updated with the latest list of publications from The Francis Frith Collection. If you wish to buy books relating to another part of the country that your local bookshop does not stock, you may purchase on-line.

For further information, trade, or author enquiries please contact us at the address below:
The Francis Frith Collection, Frith's Barn, Teffont, Salisbury, Wiltshire, England SP3 5QP.
Tel: +44 (0)1722 716 376 Fax: +44 (0)1722 716 881 Email: sales@francisfrith.co.uk

See Frith books on the internet at www.francisfrith.com

FREE PRINT OF YOUR CHOICE

Mounted Print
Overall size 14 x 11 inches (355 x 280mm)

Choose any Frith photograph in this book.
Simply complete the Voucher opposite and return it with your remittance for £3.50 (to cover postage and handling) and we will print the photograph of your choice in SEPIA (size 11 x 8 inches) and supply it in a cream mount with a burgundy rule line (overall size 14 x 11 inches).
Please note: photographs with a reference number starting with a "Z" are not Frith photographs and cannot be supplied under this offer.
Offer valid for delivery to one UK address only.

PLUS: Order additional Mounted Prints at HALF PRICE - £7.49 each (normally £14.99)
If you would like to order more Frith prints from this book, possibly as gifts for friends and family, you can buy them at half price (with no additional postage and handling costs).

PLUS: Have your Mounted Prints framed
For an extra £14.95 per print you can have your mounted print(s) framed in an elegant polished wood and gilt moulding, overall size 16 x 13 inches (no additional postage and handling required).

IMPORTANT!

These special prices are only available if you use this form to order. You must use the ORIGINAL VOUCHER on this page (no copies permitted). We can only despatch to one UK address. This offer cannot be combined with any other offer.

Send completed Voucher form to:
The Francis Frith Collection, Frith's Barn, Teffont, Salisbury, Wiltshire SP3 5QP

CHOOSE A PHOTOGRAPH FROM THIS BOOK

Voucher for **FREE** and *Reduced Price Frith Prints*

Please do not photocopy this voucher. Only the original is valid, so please fill it in, cut it out and return it to us with your order.

Picture ref no	Page no	Qty	Mounted @ £7.49	Framed + £14.95	Total Cost £
		1	Free of charge*	£	£
			£7.49	£	£
			£7.49	£	£
			£7.49	£	£
			£7.49	£	£
			£7.49	£	£
Please allow 28 days for delivery. Offer available to one UK address only			* Post & handling		£3.50
			Total Order Cost		£

Title of this book . . . .
I enclose a cheque/postal order for £ . . . .
made payable to 'The Francis Frith Collection'

OR please debit my Mastercard / Visa / Maestro card, details below

Card Number

Issue No (Maestro only)   Valid from (Maestro)

Expires   Signature

Name Mr/Mrs/Ms . . . .
Address . . . .
. . . .
. . . .
. . . . Postcode . . . .
Daytime Tel No . . . .
Email . . . .

ISBN 1-85937-450-6   Valid to 31/12/08

Can you help us with information about any of the Frith photographs in this book?

We are gradually compiling an historical record for each of the photographs in the Frith archive. It is always fascinating to find out the names of the people shown in the pictures, as well as insights into the shops, buildings and other features depicted.

If you recognize anyone in the photographs in this book, or if you have information not already included in the author's caption, do let us know. We would love to hear from you, and will try to publish it in future books or articles.

Our production team

Frith books are produced by a small dedicated team at offices in the converted Grade II listed 18th-century barn at Teffont near Salisbury, illustrated above. Most have worked with The Francis Frith Collection for many years. All have in common one quality: they have a passion for The Francis Frith Collection. The team is constantly expanding, but currently includes:

Andrew Alsop, Paul Baron, Jason Buck, John Buck, Jenny Coles, Heather Crisp, David Davies, Natalie Davis, Louis du Mont, Isobel Hall, Chris Hardwick, Julian Hight, Peter Horne, James Kinnear, Karen Kinnear, Tina Leary, Stuart Login, Sue Molloy, Sarah Roberts, Kate Rotondetto, Eliza Sackett, Terence Sackett, Sandra Sampson, Adrian Sanders, Sandra Sanger, Julia Skinner, Lewis Taylor, Will Tunnicliffe, David Turner and Ricky Williams.